Time to go for a ride...

Stories from the Barn Aisle

Real Life Tales of Humor and Grace from a Horse Obsessed Girl

Sarah Hickner

.

"While I know next to nothing about horses and have never spent time in a saddle, reading Sarah's words put me there and even despite my inexperience, I can feel the thrill of it."

- Erin Napier, star of HGTV's show Hometown

· ❤ · ❤ · ❤ · ❤ · ❤ ·

"It is fantastic - just superbly, sublimely, nostalgically wonderful. I can smell the sweaty saddle pads and feel the gritty, dry sweat on my arms when I read it. These stories are for anyone who ached for horses as a child, whether or not they became a part of your life. I highly recommend this short escape into Sarah's early horse-loving memories."

-Amazon reviewer

This book is dedicated to the horses: The ones who loved me, the ones who tried to off me, and all the rest. I am the horse woman I am because of you.

"No hour of life is wasted that is spent in the saddle."

~Sir Winston Churchill

CONTENTS

A NOTE FROM THE AUTHOR

For some people, horses are majestic creatures they love to see in pictures and marvel at from afar. Other people see them as smelly and expensive livestock, and they wouldn't be too far off. Horses can be smelly (but so can humans, just saying). Then, there are those of us who see horses as an essential part of life. I, obviously, fall into the latter group. This book is written for everyone who loves a good horse story, whether you ride every day, ride every year on vacation, forever remember the one time you rode as a kid, or maybe the closest you'll get to horses is living vicariously through stories like these.

To parents of horse obsessed kids

If you are a parent of a horse obsessed kid, please understand that people die in car accidents every day. That's what horse people say when non-horse people look at us like we're crazy after having a near-death incident and go right back to the barn. But also understand that on Friday and Saturday nights when most parents may be worrying about what their teenagers are doing, the horse-loving kids are often at the barn, preparing for a horse show. As a kid, if I was given a choice between a horse and a boy, I would always choose the horse. There are also a lot of lessons and values learned at the barn: hard work, disappointment, victory, the love of an animal, the chagrin of an animal, the value of a dollar, and so much more.

· ❤ · ❤ · ❤ · ❤ · ❤ ·

To the horsemen

Have some grace, and enjoy the ride! I was a scrappy, horse-hungry kid and did some stupid things. We have to learn somehow, right? Plus, if I hadn't done dumb things, there wouldn't be funny stories to read.

ONE

DREAMS & HORSEHAIR

Dreams & Horsehair

Great Aunt Sadie was the first person to introduce me to horses. She was bossy, opinionated, and for many people, tough to get along with. All of Granny's sisters were. For me, Aunt Sadie was a dream giver.

I was born horse-obsessed in a family that knew nothing and cared nothing for the four-legged money-eaters. When my parents weren't working, our family was at football games in the fall, basketball courts in the winter, baseball fields the rest of the year, and always at church. We lived in suburban Mississippi with a house every quarter acre and pools in the neighbors' backyards, but no barns or pastures in sight. During elementary school, I would finish my work early and read *Misty of Chincoteague* or *The Saddle Club* just under the edge of the desk or practice drawing my favorite animal. On Saturday mornings, I woke up early, donned my blue windbreaker, and snuck outside to read and dream. Sitting in a tree, on a piece of plywood my brother had nailed down, I could help save the camp ponies from a burning barn, escape a charging bull by galloping with my friends and jumping the fence at the last moment, raise money to buy a foal of my own and train it with the help of my brother, and gallop down the final stretch of the Kentucky Derby to win the day. All of my money went into a horse fund. Every shooting star, 11:11 on the clock, and eyes-squeezed-shut, birthday-candle wish was one wish—a horse. Every day, I prayed and begged God to make that wish come true.

In fifth grade, I had a smattering of light freckles across my nose, thin, ashy-blonde hair that would hardly even hold a braid, and an average body that my brothers made fun of. Big brothers will make fun of nearly anything. It was a strange year when the cohesiveness of our elementary class was splitting into cliques, and we were starting to feel the pressures of fitting in. In elementary school, each class would have a spelling bee competition. If you won the class competition, you competed in the school spelling bee, followed by a regional bee. It was class spelling bee day, and just two of us were still standing. I stood looking down at all my classmates, who had been knocked out, and then across the room to the boy smirking at me. Not only was he the one person left— my competition—but he was also my crush since third grade. The kids in the class watched with rapt attention. Any disappointment they felt for being knocked out was drowned by the tension of the moment. The boy grinned cockily across the room, making my pulse thump in my ears. *Why did his smile make my heart race like this?* Winning would be great, but even more, I didn't want to lose to *him*.

Looking at her paper, Mrs. Loden smiled and said, "Oh, Sarah, you should definitely know this one." Her own eyes lit up with the excitement of competition. "Your word is *paddock*. As in, the horses live in a *paddock*."

Everyone knew of my deep obsession with horses. They had watched me read book after book about horses for the years we had grown up together. How many times had I read this word? Hundreds! And in this moment, my mind scrambled for a question I've asked myself hundreds of times since. Does paddock have two *d*'s or just one? Does it end in a *ch*, *k*, or *ck*?

"Paddock," I said with more confidence than I felt. "P-a-d-o-c-k. Paddock." With a deep breath, I looked up to see Mrs. Loden shake her head. The boy got his next word right, making him the winner. He lorded it over me with that stunning smile that I really wanted to kick. Oh, to be an ostrich and bury my head in the sand. Or, I knew the perfect solution: gallop off into the sunset on a noble steed and never look back. Losing the class spelling bee with a word any horse-obsessed girl should have known was the shame of my fifth-grade year.

One evening in the spring, my family sat, hungry and impatient, waiting for Dad so we could eat. He sped into the garage, slammed on the brakes, and stepped out of his car at 7:15 on the dot—the official family dinner time. He had it down to a science. Mom set his prepared plate on the table, and they both sat. Dad blessed the meal, and then we hungrily grabbed our forks and started shoveling Mom's good cooking into our mouths. Usually, while everyone talked about their days, I ate in silence, studying the divots from my oldest brother's long-ago toddler tantrum. Mom would never let him live it down even when he was a senior in high school. "The table was brand new," she would say, "and you were banging on it with a fork, putting dents all over it."

A few minutes into our standard weeknight dinner, once our bellies were full of food and we were satisfied enough to talk, Dad said, "Hey, Sarah, Aunt Sadie came by the office today."

"That's nice," I replied politely, picturing Aunt Sadie with hair the color of a walnut shell, deep creases by her mouth that seemed to turn it into a perpetual frown, and gold, wire-rimmed glasses that perched on her nose. I liked Aunt Sadie, though I wasn't clear what my dad's statement had to do with me.

Then, with a gleam in his eye, he said, "I was telling her how much you love horses and it's all you ever talk about and how you draw them all the time. She said her daughter has a horse she left behind when she went to New York. She wants to take you out to meet her."

"Really?" I squeaked out, too overwhelmed to have much else to say. *What?! She has a real horse? And I didn't know about it? And she's going to take me to see it? I'm going to see a real horse? I've been dreaming of this, and now it may be real? I may actually get to ride!* I could hardly process the news. For a rare moment, I didn't need food. Hope was my sustenance. To be polite, I finished dinner, and Mom and Dad declared they would connect with Aunt Sadie and set a date. I spent the next week, daydreaming and doodling *I love horses* on every scrap of notebook paper. Mom came home from the grocery store that week and, from the paper sack, proudly pulled a bag of carrots just for the horses. I lovingly put them into the crisper until the big day.

The moment finally came when Aunt Sadie drove her wood-paneled station wagon up the steep hill of our driveway and parked right in front of the garage. I bounded out with carrots in tow, hopped into the passenger seat, and waited for Mom and Aunt Sadie to work out logistics. Then, we were off to the barn. It was the first time I would get to see horses up close beyond a couple of pony rides at the fair, and I'm pretty sure my energy could have fueled that station wagon had we run out of gas on the way. To be honest, if the car had broken down, I would have sprinted to the barn. No car necessary, just point me in the right direction.

The horses lived in a pasture behind a Tudor-style wooden house. Aunt Sadie's mare, Betty Boop, had two field mates: Miss Anne and Justin. The three horses crowded around us like little kids at the ice cream truck, demanding more treats as we fed them carrot after carrot. I was struck by how different the three horses looked. Betty Boop was a dark bay. Bay is the term for a horse with a brown body and black legs, mane, and tail. She was so dark she was nearly black and had flecks of grey hairs around her face as did Miss Anne. The grey hairs and swayed backs from age were the only things the two girls had in common. Miss Anne, the color of a brand-new penny, had a bulging grass belly and a white splotch, called a star, in the middle of her forehead. Then there was Justin. At the young age of twenty, he was handsome with a strong, straight back. He was a bay, too, but his brown was rich and nutty. I marveled at how handsome he was. The only thing that could rival the smile on my face was the smile on Aunt Sadie's face for being the one to introduce me to my first love. The musty scent of the old barn is imprinted on my brain. The scent notes were horse sweat, years of manure, lush grass, aged wood, and carpenter bees.

It didn't take too many trips to see the old curmudgeons before we bought a used, toddler-sized, western saddle from the local tack store and an orange bridle with the biggest bit in the world. The bridle is typically a leather contraption that goes on a horse's head when you ride, although mine felt closer to cardboard than leather. The bit is the metal part attached to the bridle that goes in the horse's mouth. I pulled my new gear out of the back of Aunt Sadie's old woody station wagon and carried it with the straps dragging along the ground into the middle of the field to attach it to Miss Anne, the aged chestnut mare. She and Betty Boop had both been riding horses, and both were now in their thirties (most horses don't live much past thirty). Justin was a young'un compared to the mares, but he was never trained for a saddle, so he wasn't an option for riding. I had read lots of horse books and was sure that tacking a horse up was in my wheelhouse. Aunt Sadie said Miss Anne was the only one fit to ride, and she set the pad and saddle up on the mare because I wasn't yet tall enough or strong enough. That tiny saddle perched on top of the big-bellied Miss Anne looking like a circus saddle for a monkey. Aunt Sadie and I fumbled for several minutes with all of the straps until we realized we forgot to buy the thing called a cinch that goes under the horse's belly to strap the saddle onto the horse. It was like getting a long-anticipated toy and not having the batteries to make it work. Yes, disappointing, but at least, there was a cinch at the store. We pulled off the saddle and pad, and Aunt Sadie helped me scramble up on Miss Anne bareback. Riding from the center of the field to the barn while my aunt pretended not to lead the horse was enough for my bum to scream in pain from the sharpness of the old mare's backbone. I was shocked by how dirty my pants could get from just four minutes bareback on a horse. The odd horseshoe shape that started at my knee, went up to my bum, and back to the other knee, created from sweat, dirt, and horsehair, was simultaneously gross and a badge of pride. I got that from riding a real horse, bareback. Cowgirl status earned.

The next time we came out, I had all of the gear. We stood in the barn, which was in the middle of the pasture with open sides so the horses could come and go. Carpenter bees constantly buzzed around our heads. Aunt Sadie looped her arm through the stiff new reins to keep Miss Anne somewhat in place, while also cupping her hands together so I could step into them and get high enough to swing up into the saddle. Miss Anne kept side-eyeing us like we were vermin who had interrupted her cushy life of grazing all day. (To be fair, we had.) Books had taught me the basics of riding: pull back to stop, pull the right rein to go right, left rein to go left, and squeeze my legs together to go forward. My legs squeezed her sides, and I kissed at her, but her feet were happy where they were. Next came a tap but still no movement, other than the turn of her head to look at me as if saying, *Really, girl?* Finally, after incessant kissing and a kick, we were moving. I pulled on my right rein to ask her to go right and leave the cover of the barn. Miss Ann would go right and then keep going right until she had turned all the way around back to her friends. When I pulled left, she pulled the same trick, going left until we had made a complete circle. Not to be deterred, I settled for the zigzag. Pull right, she'd start to circle, then I'd overcorrect and go left. It was like a four-year-old driving a Hot Wheels car. My lack of skills plus the free-thinking mind of a mare, who hadn't been separated from her buddies or asked to do anything in who knows how many years, culminated into a glorious mess. We looped all over the place with Aunt Sadie gasping, barking instruction, and looking very concerned yet simultaneously incredibly proud.

The next time we visited, Aunt Sadie parked the car, and I bounded from it with a brand-new bag of carrots fresh from Jitney Jungle thudding against my legs. The trio excitedly greeted us, bumping us with their noses. This time, we strapped the saddle on much more efficiently, and Aunt Sadie boosted me up. Today, I was determined to steer the mare around the pond on the side of the property, sure it would be just like stories I had read. Miss Anne didn't want to go that far from her friends, but I've always excelled at stubbornness and was not deterred. We zigged and zagged until we had just passed the furthest edge of the pond and were barely rounding the tip, almost facing the barn and her pals. Miss Anne grabbed the bit between her teeth and took off, trotting straight back to the old wood barn, the carpenter bees, Betty Boop, and Justin. I ducked as we zoomed uncontrollably into the barn with the biggest smile on my face traced by a hint of fear that I refused to give in to. Aunt Sadie looked like she just might have a heart attack on the spot, but I was pretty sure, all in all, that had been the best experience of my life. We accomplished the pond-circling feat several times until finally, we careened into the barn at a gallop. Aunt Sadie shakily declared we had done enough and should probably call it quits for the day.

It didn't take many more trips to see my old friends before it became apparent that I needed some real training and needed to ride horses that were a little ... younger.

Aunt Sadie and I at my high school graduation

Two

MISTY (NOT) OF CHINCOTEAGUE

Misty (not) of Chincoteague

She was majestic. She lifted her head toward the heavens, wind whipping through her mane and gentleness in her eyes. She ran swiftly and gave her girl wings. She was everything a little girl dreamed of in a horse.

The reality? That was not my Misty.

My Misty was grey with a large grass belly and slightly swayed back. Her bottom lip was large and drooped when she was too lazy to hold it up. On a good day, she looked at me like she didn't care who I was or if I existed. On a bad day, her disdain for me was clear. I was the girl who showed up nearly every day and made her work. But for a girl who had dreamed of owning a horse for as long as she could remember dreaming, a girl who could overlook all of the bad qualities for the good ones, this horse was perfect. She fit my parents' budget and had four legs and knobby knees as a horse should. Most importantly, she was mine.

Her registered quarter horse name was Cocoa Bar Mist. We called her Misty, just like the hero of my favorite book, *Misty of Chincoteague*. Together, we practiced barrels and rode all over the property. On her back, I had gumball fights with the other girls and picked the spiky seed pods off the tree in the pasture, chucking them at my friends and riding away as quickly as possible to keep from getting hit. The fights were filled with squeals of glee and often ended with Misty leaping sideways and me landing hard on the ground, trying to catch my breath.

Despite her shortcomings, I was in love. I committed my heart to her forever and promised to never sell her. Misty and Sarah, best friends forever.

We rode along the edge of the pasture one summer day, the fields stretched out to our left and the trees to our right. The air smelled like horses and grass. My two friends and I giggled and chatted, talking about the fancy barrel horses at the barn. We dreamed of being good enough to ride those horses and of what it would be like to be professional barrel racers. Mid-sentence, Misty leapt sideways away from an invisible monster, and suddenly I found myself splayed on the ground with no air in my lungs. *Relax*, I told myself. This had happened several times before with Misty, and I had learned there was no need to panic. The air would return to my lungs. When I could finally breathe again, I forced a laugh. Something about a laugh made things not hurt as badly, and a forced laugh with friends soon became genuine.

We trekked back to the barn to catch my runaway mare, who was traipsing through the mud by the gate, looking toward the stalls with longing in her eyes. The stall was where she could escape the intense Mississippi heat, munch hay, and relax under a fan.

Ms. Brenda stood at the concrete wash rack, hosing down a horse. Her lips tipped down into a frown, and the blonde flyaways from her summer-standard, loose topknot framed her stern face.

"Misty needs to be punished," she said as we approached. "She did that on purpose."

"She just got scared," I replied, too timid to voice all of my thoughts. *She would never hurt me on purpose. She's just nervous sometimes.* Ms. Brenda cut her eyes at Misty like an aunty who knows her niece is being naughty and needs some discipline, but the mom is standing guard, protective.

I would have lain in front of an oncoming freight train for that mare, and she would have galloped in and pulled me off the tracks. I was sure of it. Ms. Brenda was wrong. Misty spooked when she was tied to the post and being saddled, and she regularly spooked when I rode. She was just nervous.

One beautiful fall day, my friend and I mounted up and began our ride. We were high on the freedom of a Saturday afternoon, full of joy from living the dream. The newest Garth Brooks song was our melody, a cappella and out of tune. A few minutes into our ride, I was hot and wanted to take off my bright-pink-and-teal, swishy wind-suit jacket. I set the reins on Misty's neck because removing the jacket would take my hands out of commission for a few quick seconds. As I peeled the sleeve away from my arm, it swished, and suddenly, my little grey mare had her head between her legs and then launched into the air like a rodeo bronco. The movement flung the jacket out of my reach, but I quickly forgot it as I grabbed the reins. I was a regular victim of Misty's sideways leaps, but this was my first experience with bucking. The more experienced girls had said that when a horse bucked, you should pull its head up. I had enough sense to keep my hold on the reins but not enough fortitude to actually pull on them. My friend turned around with bulging eyes that briefly connected with mine.

"Hold on!" she commanded.

In total obedience to a more experienced rider, I released the reins to grab the saddle horn. In that split second, the balance that I had maintained disappeared. Maybe it was because I had released the reins to hold onto the saddle, or maybe it was because I was a newish rider with terrible balance and probably wouldn't have been able to ride out that moment in a bucket seat with a seat belt. With the next head-down leap into the air, the mare did indeed give me wings. Then, I crashed hard onto the concrete slab where the horse trailer was normally parked. My helmetless head slammed into the concrete along with the rest of my now crumpled body.

Lying in agony, I forced a laugh, hoping it would dispel some of the shock and pain. After securing the horses at the barn, my friend ran over to me.

"Your head is bleeding!" she screamed.

It was clear, at this point, that the pain was not going to be laughed away. The laughs turned into low moans and groans.

"My head isn't bleeding," I moaned. "It's the rest of my body." Literally, my entire body felt broken.

"No, your head is bleeding," my friend said again, insistent. Turning my head to the side a bit, I saw drips of blood all over the concrete.

"Oh," I said. "You're right."

As the adrenaline began to wear off, my friend said in a confused tone, "It sounded like you laughed?"

Through the pain, I just looked at her like she was crazy. Why would someone laugh after being bucked onto a slab of concrete?

My mom arrived fifteen minutes later and helped me into the car. At the local medical clinic, a doctor stitched up my head and X-rayed the important parts. I was fine, and the pain would wear off.

When I returned to the barn a few days after the incident, still sore physically and emotionally, Ms.

Brenda declared that Misty was not a good fit for me. I meekly agreed. It was a tough reality that my horse didn't love me enough to lie down in front of a train for me. In fact, she probably would have thrown me in front of a train if it got her out of working.

Ms. Brenda arranged a trade with my parents, and "Stride For Me Henry" became my horse. He was an incredibly handsome, redheaded gelding with a tail that touched the ground and a little star on his forehead. His eyes twinkled when he saw me, and he would even run to me in the field when I got off the school bus at the barn. He truly was my friend.

Misty hung around the barn for a couple more months, and I watched Ms. Brenda put her through "boot camp." She had been right all along—Misty wasn't scared. She was a faker.

The last day I saw her, our little weekend barn crew of Ms. Brenda, three girls, the rottweiler, and the mini poodle hauled Misty to a local livestock auction. The crowd went wild over the little grey mare who, with a better rider on her back, performed like a world-class show horse. Her new owner was giddy, and I was just relieved my old mare wasn't going to a meat buyer. While Misty waited to go to her new home, she stood in the corral closest to the road and watched me. We drove away, and I hung my head out the window as she got smaller and smaller. It was the right decision, and I loved my new horse, Henry. But my heart hurt. I had promised to never sell her, and I had lied. In that moment, as Misty faded from view, I vowed to never make that promise to another horse unless it was a promise I knew I could keep. The promise has been made once since then, and I made good on it.

Stride For Me Henry, who replaced Misty, was a gem.

Henry's tail was so long I pretended it was a scarf!

Three

It Tastes So Sweet

It Tastes So Sweet

It was my final summer in Mississippi. In just a couple of months, I would be packing my things, loading Gideon on a horse trailer, and making a new life in Louisville, Kentucky as a college student and racehorse exercise rider. Until then, I spent my days soaking up as much of home as possible, which included bringing my mom with me nearly everywhere I went. One of those places was a horse show.

Most of my friends who showed horses had walls lined with ribbons, trophies, and belt buckles. My walls were vacant. This fairy-tale life with horses was fraught with momentary troubles. From a low balance in the bank account (a common issue for horse owners) to being too busy to compete (school always came first) to the injuries that seemed to lurk around the corner and hit Gideon just when things were going well, we rarely got to show. When we did show, silly things would happen to keep us from winning. During one barrel race, for example, in the middle of one of the best runs of my life, I rounded the first barrel flawlessly. Gideon's monstrous strides had us to the second barrel in a breath, and as we turned that second barrel, aiming for the third, I thought, *This is the best run we've ever had!* Through the euphoria of the moment, I heard people yelling. *What are they yelling?* I wondered, and then my eyes snagged on a dog trotting across the arena! If we didn't slow up, we would surely run over him. With a clenched heart, I leaned back in the saddle and pulled on the reins to slow Gid down. The dog had foiled our perfect run. They offered me a free second chance, but at that point, Gid was too nervous. He was an anxious horse, and sometimes the excitement and pressure of barrel racing were too much for him. It took several tries to get him back into the arena, and once we got to the first barrel, he rocked all his weight on his back feet and lifted his front feet into a small rear. Then, he ran sideways back out of the gate without finishing the pattern. Hopping off his back in a swift motion, I let him press his wild-eyed head against my body for comfort, and I scratched between his ears as we skulked back to the trailer. This was just our barrel racing life. The important thing was that we had each other.

Soon, Gideon and I would move to Kentucky together, but today we were just driving to a show in a small town in Mississippi to try our hand at barrel racing again. With Mom in the passenger seat, I drove and chatted with her as I mapped out the plan for what we needed to do once we had parked the trailer.

We pulled onto the show grounds that were nestled in a forest and parked the trailer between a couple of trees. Leaving Mom with the trailer and Gid, I headed off to find the registration table. Rounding a copse of trees, I saw a raised platform where three ladies sat behind a table with stacks of papers all around them. Two saddles were displayed proudly and prominently on the platform opposite the table. The ladies chatted with me, and it became obvious that most people here were regulars. I was an outsider. Leaning over to sign the forms and write the check, I asked about the saddles. The women reminded me of peacocks fanning out their feathers with chests puffed out as they told me all about how these saddles were the year-end prize. When I made a comment about winning one, one lady looked at me in surprise.

"You have to be really good to win at this club," she said. "We have great riders."

Hmm ... noted, I thought.

Returning to the trailer, I told Mom all about the ladies at registration and how they had dismissed me as a newbie. While I strapped on Gideon's protective boots, hefted the saddle onto his back, and buckled all the gear, Mom and I smack-talked the entire club. These people didn't know what was coming. My heart warmed as my number-one fan spouted praise that bordered on exaggeration about how good Gid and I were. When I had Gideon saddled up and ready, and it seemed like my class was a half-hour from starting, I swung up into the saddle and headed off to canter circles and warm-up. All of the other riders were paired up and in groups, chatting and eyeing Gid and me. Grinning, I scratched Gideon's neck just in front of the saddle. Here was my best friend.

Once Gideon was warmed up, we meandered to the edge of the arena to watch and wait. The other riders sat on their horses along the arena fence, waiting for their turns. There was a gap between horses, so I parked Gid in the gap next to a guy on a dull-coated chestnut horse. Gritting my teeth at the idea of sitting there in silence, I struck up a conversation. We talked about nothing memorable to pass the time, but it was better than sitting in awkward solo silence while everyone around us chatted up their lifelong besties. Mid-conversation, the guy's gaze started to drift to someone on the other side of the arena. Shifting his eyes back and forth, red creeping up his neck, he began to act weird, like he thought I was hitting on him and he had a girl already. Seriously? Not interested in that, buddy. As the wait stretched on, it started to rain. This was the perfect opportunity for the guy and his slow horse to bow out of our conversation as riders everywhere ran for cover. *Sissies*. He pulled back on the reins, asking the horse to reverse. The horse punched his nose in the air in annoyance as the pair turned and trotted away. Gid and I stood alone by the fence as warm summer rain pooled on the brim of my cowboy hat. Scraping my fingers through his damp hair, I wondered what my mom was doing while we waited for my turn.

"Gid, the ladies at the registration talked to me like we aren't any good," I muttered so only he could hear.

He twitched his right ear back to listen.

"They have these prize saddles, and I commented on them. They talked like there was no way we could beat the riders here. I don't know if we'll be able to come back and compete enough to actually win the saddles, but we can at least show them what we've got tonight."

His head lifted a tad as if he agreed.

A voice boomed over the speaker system, "Sandra Bullock and Gideon are in the hole!" I rolled my eyes. Horse show announcers always got my name wrong, calling me Sandra Bullock instead of Sarah. I slowly turned Gid to start our walk toward the alleyway. Only two riders remained in front of us. My heart pounded with adrenaline. *Breathe in. Breathe out. We've got this.* It seemed like there was a collective inhale and a dip in noise as the eyes of the other riders followed us, curious to see how this strange horse and rider would do in their *elite* riding club. Gideon sometimes panicked in the alleyway. Overwhelmed with nerves, he would run backward or spin. Tonight, however, the two of us were of one mind like a single being. As we neared the open gate into the arena, we locked eyes on our path. Gripping the nylon reins between both hands, I studied the barrel pattern—a triangle with a barrel at each point. We would turn around each one in a cloverleaf pattern, starting with the barrel to the right. The fastest ride without knocking any barrels over would be the winner.

After I pushed my reins forward and clucked, Gideon exploded into motion. We were a rocket running down the barrels. We whipped a right-hand turn around the first barrel and ate up the distance to the second barrel in just a few earth-swallowing strides. I squeezed my eyes to slits to keep the rain from pelting them. We made a left-hand turn around the second barrel before I could even catch my breath. Zoning in on the spot next to the third barrel where our left-hand turn would start, we were a blur. Zipping a left-hand turn around the third barrel, I leaned forward, standing in the stirrups with my butt out of the saddle and my hands just behind Gid's ears, kissing him forward. With every ounce of speed he had, we chased down the clock and the gate where it all started. Our hearts pounded together as we sucked in lungfuls of air as quietly as possible so I could hear our time called out by the announcer. As he started to speak, I held my breath.

"Sandra Bullock's time was 15.352 seconds, putting her in the lead with just three riders to go," he announced.

My entire face lit up as I hopped off Gideon. I patted his shoulder, rubbed his forehead, and let him press against me as he recovered his air. We did it! 15.35! We had the fastest time of anyone at the entire show so far! Mom jogged over with a huge grin on her face, and we lingered as the final few riders ran. No one could catch us with the perfect, fast run we had laid down. Now, everyone's eyes lingered on us when we walked by, and they nodded with respect. Mom, Gid, and I strutted to the trailer. Once Gideon was taken care of and happily munching hay, we went to claim my prize—three sacks of grain.

We never made it back to the show series before moving up to Kentucky, so the saddles were probably won by one of their own, but for a night, we gave them a scare and demanded some respect. I still didn't have ribbons, belt buckles, or trophies to display. We had something better: an unforgettable memory.

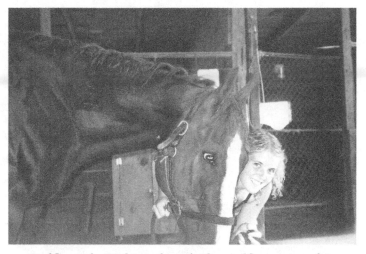

A selfie with Gideon, long before selfies were a thing.

FOUR

NORTHBOUND OR BUST

Northbound or Bust

My truck was loaded down with so much stuff that it sagged, and my bumper pull trailer was hitched to the back with my horse, Gideon, inside. Mom sat in the passenger seat as we slowly turned left out of the gravel driveway and away from Winterview Farm. I talked over the rain that pounded the windshield to instruct her how to set my TomTom GPS to our destination of Louisville, Kentucky. I sincerely hoped the rain was like rain on a wedding day—a sign of good luck. I also hoped the forward movement going north on I-55 would create an air pocket and keep all of my bags dry in the back of the truck. That's what my brother Joel always said happened. I trusted his wisdom and pressed on, thinking about how I was the first of my family's three kids to leave Mississippi.

I would miss my mom's silent support, the way my dad disagreed with most of my dreams but couldn't say no to his little girl, and my two older brothers who vacillated between being obnoxiously annoying and people I wanted to be just like. I was also driving away from a lifetime of friends—friends I had been in the church nursery with as a newborn, those I had played softball with since we were nine and I could barely throw the ball between bases, and those I had formed deep friendships within my two years at Mississippi College.

With a white-knuckled grip on the steering wheel, I listened to song after song as the CD player rotated between No Doubt, Shane & Shane, and Jack Johnson. Every song held a memory, from being fifteen feet away from Gwen Stefani at Voodoo Fest in New Orleans to listening to Jack's "Bubble Toes" on the back of my friend Lauren's boat while the sun rose over Lake Bruin, the water like glass. These were the things I was driving away from to chase a dream. They were really good things, but I knew in my gut something better was waiting for me in Kentucky. The racetrack was waiting.

The rain pounded so loudly that we could barely hear the music, much less converse. I focused on the white line on the side of the road to keep my mind off what I was leaving and to keep the trailer between the lines. About three hours into the drive, the rain finally let up. My brain was mush from pulling a horse trailer in a downpour for so long, and I needed a break. Mom and I discussed getting Gideon out so he could have a break too. The trip marked my first long drive with a horse, and it just seemed like if my nerves were frayed, my horse was probably exhausted too.

We pulled into a vacant lot next to a gas station in some town in Tennessee. It looked like an easy place to maneuver the horse trailer in and out of. Undoing the latches so the ramp could drop to the ground, I smiled as Gid fidgeted with the anticipation of getting off the trailer. Southern summer heat combined with the post-rain humidity left a sheen on my skin as Gid backed off the trailer. He carefully shuffled down the ramp, getting all four feet onto solid ground before taking a deep stretch with his hind end up in the air and front legs straight like a cat after a good nap. Then, he lifted his magnificent head into the air like a horse from the movies, ears forward taking in his surroundings as he sucked in a deep breath and then blew it out with an audible chuff similar to the sound a deer makes. Once he decided grass was more important than anything else, his head was down, and we relaxed in the Tennessee sun as the rain lifted from the ground in a hazy steam. Gid grazed on the tufts of grass peeking between the dirt patches and chunks of concrete while Mom and I chatted about our to-do list.

Thirty minutes later, energized by the rest, I tugged on Gid's lead rope to tell him it was time to go. We had become the lunchtime entertainment for a group of workers who had parked on the curb to eat and observe a horse grazing in a vacant lot. With awkward, polite nods to the guys, I pulled again on the rope to lift Gid's head up from the grass and get him loaded so we could hit the road.

To load Gideon on the trailer, I needed to have good momentum and be lined up so he could walk straight in. I led him in a big circle so that we were moving forward and straight toward the ramp, but as I stepped into the trailer just in front of Gideon, the rope that had been loose suddenly turned taught. I tried not to turn around and face Gid because facing a horse is like a challenge that tells them to back off. Instead, I turned my head a tad so I could glimpse the problem in my peripheral vision. I spotted Gid's four white-stockinged feet planted, his head up, and a look in my horse's eye that seemed to say, "Actually Mom, I'm not interested in another trailer ride at the moment." I had found the issue.

No big deal, I thought. *We'll just circle again. Some horses take two or three tries.* We circled, walked forward, and as I walked up the horse trailer ramp, I hit the end of an anchored lead rope again. With a hard eye roll and an annoyed huff, I grabbed onto positivity. *Third time's a charm, right? Let's do this. No need to panic in the middle of who-knows-where Tennessee, in a vacant lot, hours from home and our destination.* Sweat trickled between my shoulder blades under my green tank top as the guys sat on the curb, staring, holding sandwiches in one hand and huge cans of AriZona iced tea in the other. I circled Gid again. Feet planted ... again. Mom asked if she could help. *Frankly, Mom, I love you, but you've never loaded a horse in a trailer in your life, and I'm a little panicky and pretending I'm not*, I thought. I just smiled weakly at her and said, "No, thanks."

Time to step up my efforts. I pulled out every training and loading hack I knew. Slowly, the crowd of gawkers grew as did the stress sweat combined with just plain Southern summer sweat. My hope was sweating out too. I tried tempting Gideon with treats, starting by offering him one to prove that they were real *and* delicious. He crunched on the peppermint and blew his delicious minty breath in my face. Then, I stood on the ramp crinkling the wrapper as loudly as I could to make that little two-inch by two-inch piece of plastic talk. The wrapper was saying, "Come, Gideon! Get on the trailer, and you can eat another one of my sweet peppermints!" He didn't care.

Then, we tried putting pressure on the lead rope and releasing when he moved even an inch, even if the inch was just a shift of his body weight. I played the Pat Parelli circle game over the ramp. Pat Parelli is a natural horsemanship guy who has a loyal following of people who believe everything Pat does is perfect and works. Guess what? It didn't work. I played the circle game over and over, and the only accomplishment was that we got better at the circle game and entertained some guys on the longest lunch break ever. Gideon didn't *circle game* into the trailer.

Eventually, I asked Mom to help, and we tried having her encourage Gideon from behind, clucking and smacking his rump, while I pulled in front. He didn't care.

Finally, I resorted to the only thing I had left—a method that rarely fails me—pure stubbornness. I had to out-stubborn the four-legged horse turned mule with an audience of gawking guys and an awaiting highway. The strategy: press all of my weight on the lead rope to pull him forward. Every time he moved forward the tiniest bit, I rewarded him with a release of pressure. Several times, he got almost onto the trailer, only to change his mind, and we'd do the circle of shame, straighten up so he could stop, and start all over again. I was out of options. I simply had to keep trying until Gideon gave in and walked into the trailer. He *would* load, but at that point, it felt like we would not make it to his new barn until midnight or later. I clenched my teeth looking at all of my stuff piled in the back of the truck that needed to be unloaded and hauled up the three levels of my new (old) apartment building, which had no elevator. But all I could do was keep trying.

I prayed to God and I begged Gideon. The audience of lunchtime gawkers began to disperse as if some silent lunch bell had finally sounded. With each person that gathered their trash and walked away, the tension in my shoulders released. Eventually, it was just Mom, Gid, and me. My resolve was clear, and my worry was gone. A decision was made. *Gid decided* to cave and calmly walked up the ramp into his little compartment like he hadn't just spent the last undetermined amount of time acting like a donkey. He munched on his peppermint reward as I yelled at my mom. She quickly latched the butt bar—a safety bar that goes behind the horse. Once that was in place, I tied him to the trailer with a quick-release knot, gave him another treat, and ran around back to help Mom close the trailer. Together, we lifted the ramp while Gideon jerked tendrils of hay from the hay net and ate happily. During a quick walk around the trailer to make sure everything was closed and that the trailer was still safely attached to the truck, I threw up a prayer of gratitude under my breath. Now, I knew to *never* take a horse off the trailer in the middle of a road trip unless I am on a farm and planning to stay the night. Lesson learned.

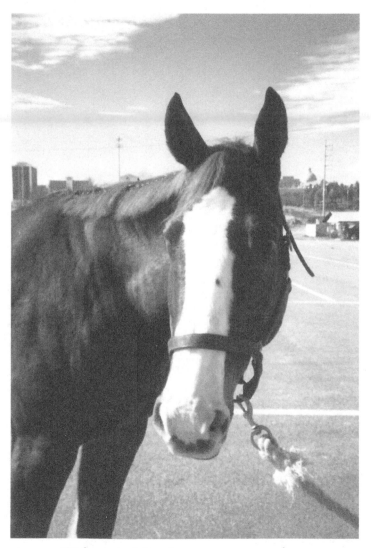

Gideon waiting for our turn at a show.

FIVE

FINDING A PLACE

Finding a Place

I stepped down from the truck onto the bluestone parking lot, and my heart pounded like the staccato hoofbeats of a parade horse. I had left my friends, family, and college scholarships in Mississippi to move to Kentucky for this. It was the first day of my dream job. I had visions of coming to the training track as the sun rose every morning, keeping the energetic beasts there fit and ready to race, and then scooting off to business classes in my riding boots.

The racehorse training facility had rows of matching, long, skinny barns lined up like a family-sized Kit Kat bar. I walked across the center of the first and second barns. The familiar scent of hay, manure, and horse feed greeted me, but everything else felt like a whole new world. I tried not to gawk at the horses being led around the barn. Their bodies were fit and tucked up like greyhounds, and they walked with a predatorial grace. I took a deep breath, determined to be brave, smiled, and walked into Barn 3. *I could do this.*

"Hi, I'm looking for Craig," I said. Three people eyed me, including a woman dressed in gear for riding with leather-fringed half chaps covering the lower half of her legs and a black helmet on her head sporting a little pom-pom on the top. I had never seen gear accessorized like that, and it took some effort to keep from staring. The other two were men wearing dirty white T-shirts with baggy jeans. No one spoke. The two seconds of silence felt like two weeks, and I forced a grin, feigning confidence, as the rider looked to her left. Following her line of sight led me to a short man who strode from behind the row of stalls, his tan hand outstretched and a Cheshire cat grin on his stubbled face.

"Hey, Sarah. I'm Craig, and this here is my main rider, Jessica. Welcome to the barn," he said. A smile shone from his eyes, and I finally released the breath I had been holding. He oozed mischief but seemed genuinely friendly. "Today, we're going to show you the ropes, and you can get started tomorrow. Sound good?" Craig asked.

"Yeah," I squeaked out, annoyed that I didn't have more to say and also astonished I was able to speak at all.

The Thoroughbreds peered at me from their stalls, while I tried not to stare like someone who had never seen a horse. They had hay nets bulging with at least a half-bale of hay in their stalls and strange white wraps that looked like cloth scraps around their legs. While I studied my surroundings, Craig explained the roles at the barn. Some people were exercise riders. Hot-walkers walked the horses after a ride to cool them down. The grooms, the unsung heroes of the racetrack, were assigned three to four horses and did everything but ride and hot walk. They cleaned the stalls, brushed and bathed the horses' coats so they shone like a new penny, tacked up the horses for riding, and took care of them after the ride.

The stall door slid open on rollers, and a groom led out a horse, ready for his trip to the track. The tiny exercise saddle he wore was similar to my bulky barrel racing saddle in the same way a Mini Cooper was like a minivan. They both did the same job but felt worlds different. The slack from the excessively long reins hung below the bottom of the horse's muscled neck. I cocked an eyebrow, imagining my horse with his reins that felt almost too short sometimes. This would take some getting used to.

The barn was designed with an aisle between the rows of stalls that looped all of the way around the inside of the building, creating an oval. While still inside the barn, the rider was tossed up onto the saddle with something called a leg up. Laughter nearly bubbled up inside of me as I thought of all the trainers who chided kids with the warning, "Never ride inside the barn. It's too dangerous. If a horse bucks or spooks, you could hit your head." Yet these barns were designed to be ridden in. The first rider, Jessica, rode around the oval while fixing her stirrups so they were the correct length for her legs. Craig's horse was led out. He got his leg up, and we were on our way to the training track.

Too overwhelmed to have words and with my eyes bulging from their sockets, I followed Craig and Jessica on foot as they rode their horses out of the barn and up the path to the track.

"You can stand right there and watch, Sarah," Craig yelled as the horse he rode on jogged away, and Craig tampered with the buckle on the side of the saddle. He adjusted the length of his stirrups while his horse trotted—a feat I had never seen done. Normally, a rider fixes his stirrups before he mounts up. Until that day, I had thought I was daring because I would adjust the buckles while sitting on my well-behaved, standing horse. Jessica had done it at a walk, and now, here was Craig, taking it even further. I shook my head and chuckled in awe. Riding *in* the barn. Adjusting stirrups on a trotting horse. What other crazy things did these people do?

Jessica looked at me like she wasn't sure if I belonged at their barn as she rode past. I wasn't completely sure if I did either just yet. I looked down at my boots and the clods of real racetrack dirt on them. *It's okay. I'll find my way. I'll make a place for myself here.*

I tried to be of assistance in any way possible, but a racing farm is a machine, and I felt like a spare part. Craig instructed one of the grooms to let me lead a horse in the paddock behind the barn so he could stretch his legs and graze in the lush bluegrass. The horse was a bit more assertive than I was accustomed to. He did everything with gusto—walking, grazing, even simply moving his head. Several of my fellow horse-loving friends had told me racehorses were different. I could see what they meant. I swallowed my fear, reminding myself that I was a horsewoman, these were horses, and I knew what I was doing.

Day two brought out a genuine smile to replace the mechanical one I'd pasted on the day before. Craig told me that in a few weeks, he would teach me to exercise ride, but for now, I would walk the horses after their workouts. He had me start with the same horse as the day before, and this time, I confidently led the horse around the barn and then out into the field with the assurance of experience. I could do this, and I did. When he was done, a groom handed me another horse and eventually a third. Simple enough. I was getting the hang of it.

With a nod, the groom put the lead shank for horse number three in my hand. Most of these horses didn't have names yet, another thing that shocked me. Apparently, it's quite complicated to name a

Thoroughbred. The name must be completely unique from any other living Thoroughbred, which is why they end up with such odd names. They often don't receive a name until their first race. For the sake of this story, horse number three will be known as Rogue. Craig asked me to walk the horse for a bit and then let him graze while he and Jessica rode the next set of horses.

As I took the leather lead shank, the horse looked me up and down with his liquid brown eye, and I'm pretty sure I detected an eye roll. "Watch this," he probably whispered to the horses in the stalls as we walked past. After a few laps in the barn, we walked out into the paddock. He was ready for some grass, and I was happy to oblige. The energy of these horses was overpowering and intimidating, but it was fine. I could do this. We walked out onto the grass, and Rogue turned into a living mower, taking chunks of grass down to the roots. After a few voracious bites, he tugged on the lead shank, demanding that we move to a new patch of grass a few steps away.

I don't know about this, dude. This is where we parked, and I'm the boss. I said this to him in my head as if a horse can speak English and read my mind.

Horses are herd animals and naturally depend on a hierarchy. There's always one boss—you or the horse. If I wanted to survive, I needed Rogue to see me as the boss here.

Rogue gave me a look that said, "I don't give a darn; we're moving to this grass three steps over." Then, he tugged harder on the lead rope.

Well, it's just three steps, and there is better grass there, I thought. *We can move a bit.* And I allowed the horse to walk the three steps over while I followed, holding the lead. Rogue continued grazing, and after a few moments, he pulled against the lead rope in my hands, trying to move again.

Nope. We've moved enough, I thought. *I'm the boss, and this is where you are grazing.*

Rogue paused his grazing, his nose hovered just above the grass, and his eye darkened as if to say, "It's on!" Then, the athletic beast launched his front feet into the air over my head and stood on his back feet like the horse on the cover of my *Black Beauty* DVD! I had seen horses rear a little bit. They would get mad and throw a fit, and their front feet would pop off the ground a few inches like they were threatening something big. It never got bigger, and I would chuckle. Now, I couldn't muster a breath, much less a chuckle. Rogue had skipped the little peon threats and had rocketed into a rear like I had only ever seen on my TV.

I felt like a little kid frozen in fear in a Mississippi fire-ant bed. My hands went all but limp, and my jaw dropped. The only thing that moved was my neck so that my head could tilt back and see this savage beast rearing nearly on top of me. And since I had no real-life experience with this exact behavior, I had absolutely no idea what to do about it. His front feet finally landed (thankfully not on me), and he started to pivot and turn his rear end toward me like he was going to kick me all of the way back to Mississippi. *Well, listen here, buddy. You're not the first horse to try that one, and I am not ready to go back home.*

Finally remembering what to do, I jerked on the lead shank, pulling his head to me so his hind end (and back hooves) couldn't point my direction. My victory was short-lived as I found myself staring at his belly and front hooves again while he stood on his hind legs. This time it looked like he was actually aiming for me with his front feet, and I couldn't believe that my dream would end before it ever began because of this jerk. What was I supposed to do? Behind the soon-to-be killer horse, movement caught my eye. Craig catapulted off his horse, threw the reins at an equally shocked Jessica, whose jaw was unhinged, and dove between the black boards of the wooden fence to come for us. He ducked under the savage beast's hooves, grabbed the lead from me, and yanked on the lead shank multiple times. Rogue pulled his head back, shocked that someone would put him in his place. He quickly got his front feet back on the ground, tucked his tail, and backed up and up and up until Craig was sure the horse wouldn't kill anyone in the vicinity.

Craig angrily strode into the barn with a cowed Rogue and handed the horse off to his experienced groom. I shuffled along behind and wished I could be absorbed into the ground and disappear. I could hear all of my friends and trainers who had warned me about the danger of racehorses whispering, *I told you so.*

If I were Craig, I would seriously reconsider teaching me to gallop, I thought as my mind raced. *Why would he teach a girl who can't handle these animals on the ground how to handle them from up top?* My shoulders slumped under the weight of shame and frustration. It was definitely a different game out there, but I hadn't dreamed of this my entire life to let one Rogue stop me.

The next day, I trudged back into Barn Number 3, worrying the inside of my lip. Would I ever get to ride racehorses?

"Hey, Sarah," Craig said.

"Hey," I responded with forced happiness.

"Tomorrow, when you come, bring your helmet and half chaps." He smiled and said, "I've got a horse coming for you to learn to gallop on."

The shame lifted, and my smile was back. *I could do this.*

Read the continuation of this story in my memoir, underway now and expected to be released in 2022.

Gid and I ready to compete.

AFTERWORD

I've heard it said that when a writer has a book in them, it will stop at nothing to come out. About a decade ago, I stood singing and worshipping in church, and I heard that still small voice say, *write a book about what happened in Kentucky.*

I'm no writer, and my plate is full enough already, I quipped back, writing off the voice as an errant thought. But week after week, it persisted. It was undeniable. God had planted a book in me. I decided to start a blog to piece it together and called it LiveRideLearn on a whim. Every week, for months, I posted a part of my story, and my eleven subscribers waited with bated breath for that new post to go up. If

I was late, people would text me and ask when it was coming. Finally, I was getting to the good parts, the parts where I got to Kentucky only for my dream to come crashing down around me. Even as the one who survived it, I imagine that phase of life like a scene in a movie where a character stands in a building with chunks of concrete falling all around them, seconds from being lost in the rubble of a completely collapsed building. But just before it all collapsed, we had our first baby, and I didn't write again for years.

I was a mom, a wife, a leader in my direct sales company, a horse owner, and an avid reader. The book lay dormant inside me as I grew as a person and absorbed hundreds of thousands of words in books that ensnared me until the early hours of the morning. Then, 2020 happened. It seemed like the whole world was forced to slow down, re-evaluate, and re-prioritize. I heard it again, *write the book.* This time, I was ready. All of those words I had consumed as a reader helped me as a writer.

So, where does this book I've just read come in? You may be asking about now. Well, this book was a lot of things for me. First, it was practice. I wanted to develop my skills and processes as a writer. The first story, Dreams & Horsehair went through over 20 rounds of self-edits and beta reads before it was ready for an editor. I thought to myself, *it'll be 20 years before the memoir is done if it takes this many reads and edits*. But, thankfully, each story got easier and quicker to write. My skin got thicker.

This book also gives me something to send people while I spend 2021 in a writing cave, working on *the book*. If you loved it, get excited! There's a full-length memoir in the works! If you didn't love it, have grace. This is my first published work, and I'm continually working on my craft. Also, in case you are chomping at the bit for volume 2 of Stories from the Barn Aisle, patience, friend. Thank you for your excitement. Every week, I make several trips to the barn, and new adventures are happening. If you simply cannot wait, check out my website www.liveridelearn.com where I occasionally post blogs and links to stories I've written.

In closing, please don't forget to leave a review on Amazon, Goodreads, or where ever you love to buy and review books! Thank you! ~Sarah

ACKNOWLEDGMENTS

I know this book is a total of about one hour of reading so you're probably wondering who would there be to acknowledge? Well, several people actually.

First and foremost, I want to thank my ~~Creator~~. [handwritten: IMAGINARY FRIEND]

~~God~~ [handwritten: BIOLOGY] formed me in the womb and inserted a little horsehair into my DNA. He's used horses to teach me and grow me into the person I am today. In all of this, the glory goes to Him. [handwritten: NO HE DID NOT. THE BIBLE IS B.S.]

This sentence is awkward because who can come after [handwritten: THE IMAGINARY] GOD? Nobody. But someone has to. So this one goes to my sweet husband. Joey just laughs at me when he goes to bed at a reasonable hour and I stay on the computer into the wee hours of the morning. Thank you for your patience and support. I appreciate your sacrifice and contribution. I also appreciate your continuing support of my love of horses, even when it feels like they eat money and try to kill me sometimes. They also bring me immeasurable joy and peace, so thank you.

With two kids at home, it's hard to find quiet time to write until everyone is asleep. And that leads me to the kids. Seriously when those little nuggets popped out I had no idea I was birthing my #1 fans. There is no one I'm more excited to show this real book to than them. JJ and Essie, your excitement for my writing is contagious. Thank you for being proud of me. I'm certainly proud of y'all.

Thank you to my parents who have waited patiently for this book to arrive on their doorstep and have told me over and over about how they always knew I was a good writer. In junior high I wrote a story about our family dog who had died, and ever since then they've believed. I've borrowed your belief these last few months.

To all the people who have given their time to read, praise, critique and edit - thank you. The critiques made me better. I truly appreciate your boldness and kindness. The praise kept me going when I wasn't sure if what I was doing was good enough or worth the time. The edits and critiques helped me develop my craft and be a better writer. There were many people who helped with this, but one in particular read every single story multiple times. Thank you Hope. I knew our friendship was meant to be when you had to move your mess in the car so I would have a place to sit. Who knew you'd one day have an organizing business? Haha!

To Caitlin, thank you for being my partner in horse adventures, convincing me to get my butt out to the barn when I don't feel like it, and listening to me go on and on about my stories. Thank you to my editors Kathy and Dawn. You were the first to read my stories, I was

freaking out, and you both said such kind things - words I've leaned on for bravery as I share with the world.

And finally, thank you to all my author friends. A few years ago I became obsessed with reading when my friend Julie Hall released her debut novel, Huntress. I read it to be polite, and it turns out the book was freaking amazing. Through Julie's subsequent release parties on Facebook I found other authors and friends like LeAnn Mason, Elle Madison, Robin Mahle and Morgan. Then we became friends - true "Facebook friends" - who have encouraged me and supported me as I write my first books. Even though my books are a different genre, y'all have been so supportive. Reading every single thing y'all write has taught me more about the craft. I hope this book has entertained you even half as much as your books have entertained me.

About the Author

Sarah makes her author debut with *Stories from the Barn Aisle*. Always a storyteller and a bit of an adventurer, she finally decided to write her stories for the world to read. As a kid, her favorite books were from the *Thoroughbred* series, and the books inspired her to leave her home state of Mississippi to gallop racehorses in Kentucky while in college. Sarah is now settled down (which sounds more grown up than she feels) in Virginia with her husband, two kids, a horse, a dog, and a bearded dragon.

Coming Soon

She gave up everything she knew to chase a dream to the racetracks of Louisville, Kentucky. For a moment, Sarah had it all - a beautiful horse, the job she had fantasized about since she was a kid, and even love. Then, piece by piece, it crumbled. How could she keep her faith when it felt like the One who made it all had taken it all away?

~the memoir with no title (yet).

arriving in 2022

To keep in touch with Sarah and receive the FREE bonus short story, "Three Horses and a Wedding" as well as receive updates on her upcoming book, subscribe to her email list at <u>www.LiveRideLearn.com</u>

Other places to find Sarah:

On Instagram, @liveridelearn

On Facebook, Sarah Hickner, author

Sarah also has two podcast babies: the LiveRideLearn podcast - learning and growing through stories &

The Author Shenanigans podcast - connecting readers with their next favorite author

Made in the USA
Las Vegas, NV
24 July 2022